CHRISTMAS CAROLS FOR TWO

Arrangements by Mark Phillips

ISBN 978-1-5400-2917-1

Contact Us:
Hal Leonard
7777 West Bluemound Road
Milwaukee, WI 53213
Email: info@halleonard.com

In Europe contact:
Hal Leonard Europe Limited
Distribution Centre, Newmarket Road
Bury St Edmunds, Suffolk, IP33 3YB
Email: info@halleonardeurope.com

In Australia contact:
Hal Leonard Australia Pty. Ltd.
4 Lentara Court
Cheltenham, Victoria, 3192 Australia
Email: info@halleonard.com.au

CONTENTS

ANGELS WE HAVE HEARD ON HIGH

ALTO SAXES

Traditional French Carol

Moderately

AWAY IN A MANGER

ALTO SAXES

Music by James R. Murray

Moderately

BRING A TORCH, JEANNETTE, ISABELLA

ALTO SAXES

17th Century French Provençal Carol

Moderately slow, in 1

DECK THE HALL

ALTO SAXES

Traditional Welsh Carol

Brightly

THE FIRST NOEL

ALTO SAXES

17th Century English Carol
Music from W. Sandys' *Christmas Carols*

GO, TELL IT ON THE MOUNTAIN

ALTO SAXES

African-American Spiritual

GOD REST YE MERRY, GENTLEMEN

ALTO SAXES

Traditional English Carol

Moderately fast

HARK! THE HERALD ANGELS SING

ALTO SAXES

Music by Felix Mendelssohn-Bartholdy
Arranged by William H. Cummings

Brightly

IT CAME UPON THE MIDNIGHT CLEAR

ALTO SAXES

Music by Richard Storrs Willis

Moderately slow, in 2

JINGLE BELLS

ALTO SAXES

Words and Music by J. Pierpont

Brightly, in 2

JOLLY OLD ST. NICHOLAS

ALTO SAXES

Traditional 19th Century American Carol

Brightly, in 2

JOY TO THE WORLD

ALTO SAXES

Music by George Frideric Handel
Adapted by Lowell Mason

Moderately, in 2

O CHRISTMAS TREE

ALTO SAXES

Traditional German Carol

Moderately

O COME, ALL YE FAITHFUL

ALTO SAXES

Music by John Francis Wade

Moderately

O COME, O COME, EMMANUEL

ALTO SAXES

15th Century French Melody
Adapted by Thomas Helmore

Moderately slow, in 2

O HOLY NIGHT

ALTO SAXES

Music by Adolphe Adam

Moderately slow, in 2

O LITTLE TOWN OF BETHLEHEM

ALTO SAXES

Music by Lewis H. Redner

SILENT NIGHT

ALTO SAXES

Music by Franz X. Gruber

Moderately

STILL, STILL, STILL

ALTO SAXES

Salzburg Melody, c.1819

Moderately slow

WE THREE KINGS OF ORIENT ARE

ALTO SAXES

Words and Music by John H. Hopkins, Jr.

Slowly, in 2

WE WISH YOU A MERRY CHRISTMAS

ALTO SAXES

Traditional English Folksong

WHAT CHILD IS THIS?

ALTO SAXES

16th Century English Melody